LATHER, RINSE, SUCCEED

Master The Art Of Mobile Car Detailing

Randy Volson

Icon Publications Limited

CONTENTS

INTRODUCTION

"Welcome to the world of possibilities where your passion for cars meets the realm of entrepreneurship. In
"Lather, Rinse, Succeed: Master The Art of Mobile Car Detailing," we invite you to embark on an exciting journey that combines your love for automobiles with the art of business building. This book is your gateway to the ins and outs of launching and thriving in the mobile car detailing industry.

From polishing your business idea to crafting a detailed plan, from mastering the art of customer service to harnessing the power of technology, this guide is a compass that navigates you through the twists and turns of entrepreneurship. Whether you're a car enthusiast looking to turn your passion into profit or an aspiring business owner seeking to enter a dynamic market, our book offers the wisdom, strategies, and actionable steps to accelerate your journey toward success.

Through a blend of practical advice, real-world examples, and expert insights, we're here to equip you with the knowledge and confidence needed to make your mobile car detailing venture shine. So, fasten your seatbelt, ignite your entrepreneurial spirit, and let's hit the road to build a thriving business that reflects your passion and aspirations. Your journey to becoming a trailblazer in the mobile car detailing industry starts now."

CHAPTER 1: INTRODUCTION TO MOBILE CAR DETAILING

Understanding The Concept Of Mobile Car Detailing

Mobile car detailing refers to a specialized automotive service where trained professionals provide a comprehensive cleaning, restoration, and maintenance process for vehicles, all within the convenience of the customer's chosen location. Unlike traditional car washes, which focus primarily on surface cleaning, mobile car detailing goes beyond by addressing both the exterior and interior aspects of the vehicle.

This service typically involves a range of meticulous tasks, including but not limited to washing, waxing, polishing, interior vacuuming, steam cleaning, leather conditioning, and more. Mobile car detailing experts often bring their own equipment, water supply, and eco-friendly cleaning products to ensure a high-quality outcome without any inconvenience to the vehicle owner.

By delivering this service directly to the customer's doorstep, mobile car detailing eliminates the need for vehicle owners to travel to a physical location, saving them time and effort. Additionally, the personalized attention and care given to each vehicle contribute to the restoration of its original appearance and condition.

In essence, mobile car detailing combines the convenience of on-site service with the expertise of detailing professionals, resulting in a thorough and personalized automotive rejuvenation experience for vehicle owners.

The Benefits Of A Mobile Business Model

The mobile business model in the context of mobile car detailing offers several advantages:

Convenience: Mobile car detailing brings the service directly to customers' preferred locations, eliminating the need for them to drive to a physical shop. This convenience appeals to busy individuals who value their time and prefer to have tasks done at their convenience.

Time Savings: Customers save time by avoiding trips to a detailing facility. They can continue with their daily activities while their vehicle is being detailed nearby, resulting in increased efficiency.

Personalized Service: With mobile car detailing, professionals focus solely on one vehicle at a time. This allows for a higher level of attention to detail and customization based on the specific needs and preferences of each customer.

Quality and Expertise: Mobile detailing experts typically bring their own specialized equipment and eco-friendly products. This ensures a higher level of quality and expertise compared to some traditional car washes that might use generic products.

Tailored Packages: Mobile car detailing often offers a range of packages that customers can choose from, allowing them to select the level of service that fits their budget and requirements.

Minimal Disruption: Customers can have their vehicles detailed at home or work, reducing disruption to their routines. They can oversee the process and ensure their vehicle's safety and security.

Eco-Friendly Options: Many mobile detailing services prioritize environmentally friendly cleaning products and water-saving techniques, making them an attractive option for environmentally conscious consumers.

Building Trust: The direct interaction between the detailing professional and the customer fosters a sense of trust and transparency, as customers can see the work being done and discuss their preferences directly.

Word-of-Mouth Marketing: Satisfied customers are likely to share their positive experiences with friends and family, leading to organic word-of-mouth marketing that can help grow the mobile detailing business.

Flexibility: The mobile business model allows for flexible scheduling and adaptability to various locations, events, and seasons. This can help maximize business opportunities throughout the year.

In essence, the mobile business model for car detailing capitalizes on convenience, personalized service, and quality to provide a unique and customer-centric experience that sets it apart from traditional brick-and-mortar operations.

Exploring The Current Market Trends And Opportunities

To explore current market trends and opportunities in the mobile car detailing industry, consider the following steps:

Industry Research: Start by researching the current state of the mobile car detailing industry. Look for reports, articles, and market analyses that provide insights into market size, growth rates, and emerging trends.

Competitor Analysis: Identify existing mobile car detailing businesses in your region. Analyze their services, pricing, customer reviews, and any unique selling propositions they offer. This can help you understand your competition and find gaps in the market.

Customer Demographics: Study the preferences and behaviors of your potential customers. Determine the types of vehicles they own, their location, income level, and their preferences for convenience and personalized service.

Technological Advances: Investigate technological advancements in car detailing equipment, products, and techniques. Stay updated on innovations that could improve the quality and efficiency of your services.

Online Presence: Examine the online presence of mobile car detailing businesses, including their websites, social media accounts, and customer interactions. This can give you insights into how they market their services and engage with customers.

Networking: Attend industry events, trade shows, and local business networking events. These gatherings provide opportunities to connect with other professionals, learn from experts, and stay informed about the latest trends.

Customer Feedback: Gather feedback from vehicle owners through surveys or online platforms. Understand their pain points, preferences, and suggestions to tailor your services to their needs.

Licensing and Regulations: Familiarize yourself with any licenses, permits, or regulations that may apply to your mobile car detailing business. Compliance is crucial for a smooth operation.

Partnerships: Explore potential partnerships with other businesses, such as local car dealerships, rental agencies, or auto repair shops. These collaborations can help you tap into new customer segments.

Economic Indicators: Keep an eye on economic indicators that might influence consumer spending on luxury services like car detailing. Understanding economic trends can help you anticipate fluctuations in demand.

Online Search Trends: Use tools like Google Trends to identify popular search terms related to mobile car detailing. This can give you insights into what potential customers are looking for.

Innovation Opportunities: Identify areas where you can innovate within the industry. This could be related to service offerings, sustainability initiatives, or customer experience enhancements.

By combining these research methods, you can gain a comprehensive understanding of the current market landscape, identify trends, and uncover opportunities that will guide your mobile car detailing business toward success.

* * *

CHAPTER 2: BUILDING THE FOUNDATION

Crafting A Solid Business Plan For Your Mobile Car Detailing Venture

Crafting a robust business plan for your mobile car detailing venture involves several key steps. Here's a guide to help you get started:

Executive Summary: Begin with a concise overview of your business, highlighting your business concept, goals, target market, and competitive edge.

Business Description: Provide a detailed explanation of your mobile car detailing business, including the services you'll offer, your value proposition, and how you'll differentiate yourself in the market.

Market Analysis: Conduct thorough research on the mobile car detailing industry. Analyze market trends, customer demographics, and competitor landscape to understand the demand and potential for growth.

Target Audience: Define your ideal customers, including their characteristics, preferences, and pain points. This will help you tailor your services to meet their specific needs.

Service Offerings: Outline the range of detailing services you'll provide, from exterior washing and waxing to interior cleaning and restoration. Clearly define each service and its associated pricing.

Marketing Strategy: Describe how you'll attract and retain customers. Outline your online and offline marketing tactics, such as social media marketing, local advertising, partnerships, and referral programs.

Operational Plan: Detail how your mobile car detailing services will be delivered. Include information about your service vehicle, equipment, scheduling, and any subcontractors or employees you plan to hire.

Financial Projections: Provide a realistic financial forecast for the first few years of your business. Include startup costs, monthly expenses, projected revenue, and profitability estimates.

Pricing Strategy: Explain how you'll determine your pricing structure. Consider factors like service complexity, market rates, and customer willingness to pay.

SWOT Analysis: Evaluate your business's strengths, weaknesses, opportunities, and threats. This analysis can guide your decisions and help you address potential challenges.

Legal and Regulatory Considerations: Outline any licenses, permits, insurance coverage, or other legal requirements specific to your location and industry.

Risk Management: Identify potential risks that could affect your business, such as seasonal fluctuations in demand, equipment breakdowns, or economic downturns. Develop strategies to mitigate these risks.

Sustainability and Environmental Practices: If relevant, highlight any eco-friendly practices you'll adopt in your detailing process. This can appeal to environmentally conscious customers.

Exit Strategy: While not always necessary, having a plan for how you might exit the business in the future (e.g., selling, merging, or passing it on) shows long-term planning.

Appendices: Include any additional information that supports your business plan, such as market research data, competitor analyses, and detailed financial spreadsheets.

Crafting a solid business plan requires thorough research, thoughtful analysis, and a clear vision for your mobile car detailing venture. This plan will serve as a roadmap for your business's success and help you secure funding, if needed.

Defining Your Business Goals And Objectives

Defining clear and achievable business goals and objectives for your mobile car detailing venture is crucial for setting a strategic direction. Here's a step-by-step approach to help you establish your goals:

Vision Statement: Start by outlining your long-term vision for the business. Envision what you want your mobile car detailing venture to become in the next 5 to 10 years. This overarching vision will guide your goal-setting process.

Mission Statement: Define the purpose and mission of your business. Explain why you're entering the mobile car detailing industry, what value you aim to provide to customers, and how you plan to stand out from the competition.

SMART Goals: Create SMART (Specific, Measurable, Achievable, Relevant, Time-bound) goals that are clear and actionable. For instance, set objectives like increasing customer bookings by a certain percentage within the first year or achieving a specific monthly revenue target.

Prioritize Goals: Identify the most important goals that align with your business's growth and development. It's advisable to focus on a few key objectives that you can realistically work towards.

Quantitative and Qualitative Metrics: Determine the metrics you'll use to measure your progress towards each goal. These could include financial metrics (revenue, profit margins), operational metrics (customer retention rate, service completion time), and customer satisfaction metrics (online reviews, feedback surveys).

Market Considerations: Align your goals with market trends and opportunities you've identified during your market research. For instance, if there's a growing demand for eco-friendly services, a goal related to sustainability could be relevant.

Short-Term and Long-Term Goals: Set a mix of short-term and long-term goals. Short-term goals could focus on immediate milestones, while long-term goals might encompass broader achievements, such as expanding your service area or introducing new service packages.

Flexibility and Adaptability: Keep your goals flexible enough to adapt to changing circumstances and industry trends. Regularly review and adjust your goals based on new insights or unexpected challenges.

Challenging Yet Attainable: While goals should be ambitious, they should also be achievable. Setting unrealistic goals can lead to frustration and burnout.

Employee Involvement: If you plan to have employees, involve them in the goal-setting process. Their insights and feedback can contribute to a more comprehensive approach.

Communication: Ensure that your team is aware of the established goals and understands their role in achieving them. Regularly communicate progress and celebrate milestones to maintain motivation.

Regular Review: Schedule regular reviews to track your progress toward each goal. This allows you to make informed decisions and adjustments as needed.

By following these steps, you'll be able to define business goals and objectives that guide your mobile car detailing venture toward success while remaining adaptable to changes in the market and industry.

Conducting Market Research To Identify Target Customers And Competitors

Here's a step-by-step approach to conducting effective market research for your mobile car detailing business:

Define Research Objectives: Clarify what you want to achieve with your market research. Identify specific goals, such as understanding customer preferences, assessing demand, and analyzing the competitive landscape.

Identify Target Audience: Determine the characteristics of your ideal customers. Consider factors like demographics (age, gender, location), psychographics (lifestyle, preferences), and behavior (vehicle ownership, frequency of detailing).

Utilize Online Tools: Leverage online resources like market research reports, industry publications, and databases to gather data on the mobile car detailing industry. These sources often provide insights into market trends, growth projections, and consumer behavior.

Competitor Analysis: Identify existing mobile car detailing businesses in your area. Evaluate their services, pricing, customer reviews, and online presence to understand their strengths and weaknesses.

Customer Surveys: Create surveys to gather direct feedback from potential customers. Ask about their car detailing preferences, pain points, and willingness to use a mobile service. Online survey platforms can help you collect and analyze responses.

Focus Groups or Interviews: Consider conducting focus groups or one-on-one interviews with individuals who match your target audience. This qualitative approach can provide deeper insights into their needs and preferences.

Online Search Trends: Use tools like Google Trends to identify popular search terms related to mobile car detailing in your region. This can give you insights into customer interests and concerns.

Social Media Analysis: Analyze social media platforms to understand conversations, reviews, and comments related to mobile car detailing services. This can reveal customer sentiments and preferences.

Networking and Events: Attend local networking events, car shows, and industry gatherings. Engage with potential customers and industry professionals to gain insights into local demand and expectations.

Local Business Directories: Explore local business directories to identify potential competitors and gather information about their services and customer reviews.

Government Data: Utilize government sources for demographic and economic data related to your target area. This can provide insights into the potential customer base and its purchasing power.

Customer Reviews and Testimonials: Analyze online reviews and testimonials for existing mobile car detailing businesses. Pay attention to what customers appreciate and what aspects they feel could be improved.

SWOT Analysis: Conduct a SWOT analysis (Strengths, Weaknesses, Opportunities, Threats) for your own business and your competitors. This can help you identify gaps in the market and areas where you can excel.

Market Size and Demand: Estimate the potential market size by considering the number of vehicles in your target area and the frequency at which car owners might require detailing services.

By following these steps, you'll gather valuable insights that will help you identify your target customers' preferences, needs, and behaviors, as well as understand the competitive landscape in the mobile car detailing industry. This information will enable you to tailor your services and marketing strategies effectively.

* * *

CHAPTER 3: NAVIGATING LEGAL AND REGULATORY ASPECTS

Registering Your Business And Obtaining Necessary Licenses

Registering your mobile car detailing business and obtaining the necessary licenses involves several steps. Here's a guide to help you through the process:

Choose a Business Structure: Decide on a suitable business structure, such as a sole proprietorship, partnership, LLC, or corporation. Each structure has different legal and tax implications.

Business Name: Select a unique and appropriate name for your business. Check with your local business registry or state agency to ensure the name is available and doesn't infringe on trademarks.

Business Registration: Register your business with the appropriate government agency. This might involve filing paperwork with your county clerk's office or state business registration agency.

EIN/Tax ID: Obtain an Employer Identification Number (EIN) from the IRS. This is necessary for tax purposes, even if you don't plan to hire employees.

Local Permits and Licenses: Check with your city, county, or municipality to identify the necessary local permits and licenses for operating a mobile car detailing business. This might include a general business license or a specific mobile business permit.

State Licenses: Depending on your location and the services you provide, you might need state-level licenses or certifications. Research your state's requirements for auto detailing services.

Environmental Permits: If you plan to dispose of waste water or use chemicals, you might need environmental permits. These ensure compliance with regulations related to water pollution and hazardous materials.

Home Occupation Permits: If you plan to operate the business from your home, you might need a home occupation permit. Check local zoning regulations to determine if this is necessary.

Sales Tax Permit: If your state imposes sales tax on services, you'll need a sales tax permit. This allows you to collect and remit sales tax on your services.

Insurance: Obtain liability insurance to protect your business from potential claims or accidents that could occur during your detailing services.

Health and Safety Regulations: If you plan to use cleaning products, ensure that you comply with health and safety regulations. This might include proper storage, handling, and disposal practices.

Trade Organization Memberships: Consider joining trade organizations related to auto detailing. These memberships can provide valuable resources, networking opportunities, and insights into industry best practices.

Contractor's License: If your detailing services involve more extensive work such as paint correction, you might need a contractor's license. Check your state's requirements.

Business Regulations: Research any specific regulations that might apply to mobile businesses, such as restrictions on operating in certain areas or during certain hours.

Renewals and Compliance: Be aware of renewal deadlines for licenses and permits. Additionally, ensure that you stay compliant with any ongoing requirements or changes in regulations.

It's important to conduct thorough research and consult with legal professionals or business advisors to ensure you have the correct licenses and permits for your mobile car detailing business. This will help you avoid legal issues and operate your business smoothly.

Understanding Environmental Regulations And Waste Disposal

Understanding environmental regulations and waste disposal for your mobile car detailing business is essential to operate in an environmentally responsible manner. Here's a step-by-step approach to help you navigate this aspect:

Research Local Regulations: Begin by researching local, state, and federal environmental regulations that apply to car detailing businesses. Look into regulations related to water usage, chemical handling, waste disposal, and pollution prevention.

Water Runoff Management: Learn about regulations governing the discharge of wastewater from your detailing activities. Some areas might have restrictions on discharging soapy water into storm drains. Explore eco-friendly water recycling options.

Chemical Handling: Understand how to properly store, handle, and dispose of cleaning chemicals, solvents, and other products you'll use. Consult Material Safety Data Sheets (MSDS) for guidance on safe usage.

Hazardous Waste Identification: Determine if any waste generated during detailing qualifies as hazardous waste. Properly identify, label, and separate hazardous waste from regular waste to ensure compliant disposal.

Waste Disposal Methods: Research approved methods for disposing of waste, including chemicals, used oils, and contaminated materials. This might involve partnering with waste disposal companies or facilities.

Recycling Opportunities: Explore recycling options for materials like plastics, glass, and metal that you might encounter during detailing. Consider recycling used oils if applicable.

Training and Education: Provide proper training to yourself and any employees about environmentally friendly practices, waste handling, and disposal methods. This ensures everyone understands their responsibilities.

Eco-Friendly Products: Choose cleaning products that are eco-friendly and biodegradable. This reduces the environmental impact of your detailing activities and is often appreciated by environmentally conscious customers.

Disposal Facilities: Identify authorized facilities where you can dispose of hazardous waste, used oils, and other materials. Establish a relationship with these facilities to ensure proper disposal.

Wastewater Management: Explore options for containing and properly disposing of wastewater generated during your detailing process. Consider using containment mats and vacuum systems to prevent runoff.

Permits and Reporting: If required, obtain necessary permits for wastewater discharge or hazardous waste handling. Understand reporting requirements to stay compliant.

Consult Experts: Consider consulting with environmental experts or waste management professionals to ensure you're adhering to regulations and best practices.

Regular Updates: Stay informed about any changes or updates to environmental regulations that might affect your business. Regularly review resources provided by local environmental agencies.

Audit and Self-Assessment: Periodically assess your waste disposal practices and environmental compliance. This helps you identify areas for improvement and ensures ongoing adherence to regulations.

Documentation: Keep records of your waste disposal processes, training efforts, and any permits you obtain. Documentation serves as proof of your commitment to compliance.

By following these steps, you can ensure that your mobile car detailing business operates in a manner that respects environmental regulations and contributes to sustainable practices. This not only benefits the environment but also enhances your reputation as a responsible business owner.

Liability And Insurance Considerations For Mobile Detailing Operations

Understanding liability and insurance considerations is crucial for your mobile car detailing business. Here's a guide to help you navigate this aspect:

Research Insurance Types: Familiarize yourself with the types of insurance that are relevant to mobile detailing operations. This might include general liability insurance, commercial auto insurance, and potentially professional liability insurance.

General Liability Insurance: General liability insurance provides coverage for bodily injury, property damage, and advertising injury claims that might arise from your business activities. It helps protect you from legal and financial repercussions.

Commercial Auto Insurance: Since you'll be operating a mobile business, commercial auto insurance is essential. It covers vehicles used for business purposes, including accidents, damage, and liability.

Professional Liability Insurance: Also known as errors and omissions insurance, this coverage protects you from claims related to professional mistakes or negligence. It's particularly relevant if you offer specialized detailing services.

Coverage Limits: Determine the appropriate coverage limits for your insurance policies. The coverage amount should be sufficient to cover potential claims and liabilities.

Workers' Compensation Insurance: If you have employees, workers' compensation insurance might be required. It covers medical expenses and lost wages for employees who are injured while working.

Talk to Insurance Experts: Consult insurance professionals or brokers who specialize in small businesses or auto-related operations. They can help you understand your specific insurance needs and recommend suitable policies.

Comparative Shopping: Get quotes from multiple insurance providers to compare coverage options, premiums, and deductibles. This helps you find the best value for your needs.

Policy Inclusions and Exclusions: Carefully review policy inclusions and exclusions to understand what is covered and what isn't. Be aware of any limitations that might affect your business.

Umbrella Insurance: Consider umbrella insurance as an additional layer of protection. It provides extra coverage beyond the limits of your primary insurance policies.

Risk Mitigation: Implement risk management practices to minimize the likelihood of accidents or incidents. Proper training, safety protocols, and careful handling of chemicals can reduce risks.

Legal Consultation: Consult legal professionals who specialize in insurance and liability to ensure you fully understand your obligations and protections.

Policy Renewals and Updates: Regularly review and update your insurance policies to reflect changes in your business operations, staff, or services offered.

Documentation: Keep copies of your insurance policies and related documents in a secure location. This makes it easy to access important information when needed.

Educate Employees: If you have employees, educate them about safety protocols, proper handling of equipment, and adherence to guidelines to minimize risks.

By following these steps, you can ensure that your mobile car detailing business is adequately protected against potential liabilities and risks. Comprehensive insurance coverage gives you peace of mind and safeguards your business's financial stability.

* * *

CHAPTER 4: ESSENTIAL EQUIPMENT AND SUPPLIES

Identifying The Must-Have Tools For A Mobile Detailing Setup

Identifying the essential tools for a mobile car detailing setup is crucial for a successful venture. Here's a guide to help you determine the must-have tools:

Vehicle: A reliable vehicle to transport your equipment and reach customers' locations is the cornerstone of your mobile detailing setup.

Water Supply: Ensure access to a clean water source, whether it's a water tank installed in your vehicle or arrangements with clients for water hookup.

Pressure Washer: A pressure washer with adjustable settings allows you to effectively clean surfaces, remove dirt, and prep vehicles for detailing.

Generator: A portable generator provides power for equipment like pressure washers, vacuums, and lighting when you're at locations without electrical outlets.

Vacuum Cleaner: A high-quality wet/dry vacuum cleaner is essential for thorough interior cleaning, removing debris, and detailing upholstery.

Steam Cleaner: A steam cleaner is versatile for sanitizing interiors, cleaning hard-to-reach areas, and removing stubborn stains.

Buffers and Polishers: These tools are crucial for applying wax, polish, and sealants, as well as restoring paint finish and removing imperfections.

Microfiber Towels: Stock up on microfiber towels for various detailing tasks, including drying, wiping, and applying products.

Brushes and Applicators: Different types of brushes and applicators help you clean intricate parts, apply products evenly, and detail hard-to-reach areas.

Cleaning Products: Invest in high-quality, eco-friendly cleaning products for various surfaces like paint, glass, tires, and interiors.

Clay Bar Kit: A clay bar kit helps remove contaminants from the vehicle's surface, leaving it smooth and ready for waxing.

Interior Cleaning Products: Get specific products for upholstery, carpets, leather, and plastics to effectively clean and condition vehicle interiors.

Tire and Wheel Cleaning Tools: Brushes, cleaners, and detailing products designed for tires and wheels enhance the vehicle's overall appearance.

Detailing Lights: Proper lighting is essential for detecting imperfections and ensuring a thorough detailing job, especially in low-light conditions.

Organization and Storage: Invest in storage solutions like shelves, compartments, and toolboxes to keep your equipment organized in your vehicle.

Safety Equipment: Consider items like gloves, safety glasses, and protective clothing to ensure your safety during detailing tasks.

Mobile Payment System: Set up a mobile payment system to accept payments from clients on-site using credit cards or mobile apps.

Customer Interaction Tools: Have business cards, brochures, and appointment scheduling tools to communicate effectively with customers.

Environmental Products: Offer eco-friendly options for customers who prioritize sustainability.

First Aid Kit: Keep a basic first aid kit in your vehicle to address minor injuries or accidents.

To identify the must-have tools for your mobile car detailing setup, consider the specific services you plan to offer, the types of vehicles you'll work on, and the preferences of your target customers. As your business grows, you can expand your toolkit to meet evolving needs and offer more specialized services.

Selecting High-Quality Cleaning Products And Solutions

Selecting high-quality cleaning products and solutions is essential for delivering exceptional results in your mobile car detailing business. Here's a step-by-step guide to help you make the best choices:

Research Trusted Brands: Start by researching reputable brands that specialize in automotive cleaning and detailing products. Look for brands with a track record of producing effective and reliable solutions.

Read Reviews and Recommendations: Read customer reviews and seek recommendations from fellow detailers or professionals in the industry. Honest feedback can provide insights into the performance of different products.

Consider Product Specializations: Different cleaning products are designed for specific surfaces and materials. Consider products that cater to different vehicle parts such as paint, glass, tires, upholstery, and leather.

Check Ingredients: Examine the ingredients of cleaning products to ensure they are safe for the vehicle's surfaces and the environment. Avoid products with harsh chemicals that might cause damage.

Look for Certifications: Some cleaning products carry certifications indicating they are eco-friendly, biodegradable, or safe for certain materials. Look for seals of approval from recognized organizations.

Test Small Samples: Before committing to bulk purchases, consider buying small sample sizes to test the products on a limited area of a vehicle. This helps you assess their effectiveness and compatibility.

Product Versatility: Opt for versatile products that can handle multiple tasks. For example, an all-purpose cleaner can be used on various surfaces, reducing the number of products you need to carry.

Product Performance: Research how well products perform in terms of cleaning, removing stains, and enhancing the vehicle's appearance. Look for products that offer superior results.

Ease of Use: Choose products that are easy to apply and remove. Products that require minimal effort to achieve desired results can improve your efficiency.

Availability and Pricing: Consider the availability of the products in your region and compare prices. While quality is important, finding products that fit your budget is also crucial for profitability.

pH Balance: pH-neutral products are generally safer for vehicle surfaces and less likely to cause damage. They help maintain the integrity of paint, plastics, and other materials.

Packaging and Dispensing: Look for products with convenient packaging and dispensing methods. Pump sprays, trigger sprays, and aerosols can make application easier.

Manufacturer's Recommendations: Follow the manufacturer's recommendations for product application, dilution ratios, and safety precautions.

Customer Support: Consider brands that offer good customer support in case you have questions about product usage or issues.

Start Small and Grow: Begin with a basic set of cleaning products and gradually expand your range as you gain experience and understand the specific needs of your customers.

By carefully evaluating these factors and conducting thorough research, you can select high-quality cleaning products and solutions that will contribute to the success and reputation of your mobile car detailing business.

Choosing The Right Vehicle For Your Mobile Business

Selecting the right vehicle for your mobile car detailing business is a crucial decision that can impact the efficiency and professionalism of your operations. Here's a step-by-step approach to guide you through the process:

Assess Business Needs: Consider the scope of your mobile detailing services. Determine the equipment, tools, and products you'll need to carry and whether you'll offer specialized services.

Vehicle Size and Type: Choose a vehicle that offers sufficient space for storing your equipment and tools while allowing you to move comfortably. Options include vans, trucks, SUVs, or even trailers.

Fuel Efficiency: Opt for a vehicle with good fuel efficiency to help manage operational costs. Mobile detailing involves driving to various locations, so fuel efficiency can impact profitability.

Payload Capacity: Ensure the vehicle can handle the weight of your equipment, water tanks, generators, and other tools without straining its payload capacity.

Vehicle Condition: Select a vehicle in good condition to minimize maintenance and repair costs. Consider purchasing a new or gently used vehicle to reduce the likelihood of breakdowns.

Customization Options: Look for vehicles that can be customized or retrofitted to accommodate your detailing equipment. Shelving, storage compartments, and interior modifications can enhance organization.

Reliability and Brand: Opt for reputable brands known for reliability and durability. Research vehicle reviews and reliability ratings to make an informed decision.

Vehicle Maintenance: Consider the ease of maintenance and availability of parts for the chosen vehicle. Regular maintenance is essential to keep your mobile detailing business running smoothly.

Insurance Costs: Check with insurance providers to estimate insurance costs for the vehicle you're considering. Insurance premiums can vary based on the type and model of the vehicle.

Budget Considerations: Set a budget for the vehicle purchase, factoring in both the vehicle cost and potential modifications. Ensure the chosen vehicle aligns with your budget.

Vehicle Age: Balance between cost and age. While newer vehicles might come with warranties and modern features, slightly older models might offer better value.

Appearance and Branding: Choose a vehicle that aligns with your business's professional image. Consider how you'll brand the vehicle with your business name, logo, and contact information.

Test Drive: Whenever possible, schedule a test drive to assess the vehicle's comfort, handling, and performance. This can help you evaluate its suitability for your business.

Resale Value: Research the resale value of the vehicle model you're considering. Resale value can impact your ability to upgrade or replace the vehicle in the future.

Consider Future Growth: Plan for future growth by selecting a vehicle that can accommodate expanding equipment and service offerings.

By considering these factors and conducting thorough research, you can choose a vehicle that aligns with your mobile car detailing business's needs, enhances your efficiency, and projects a professional image to your clients.

* * *

CHAPTER 5: SETTING UP YOUR MOBILE WORKSPACE

Designing An Efficient And Organized Workspace Within Your Vehicle

Designing an efficient and organized workspace within your mobile car detailing vehicle is essential for maximizing productivity and delivering professional services. Here's a step-by-step approach to help you create an effective workspace:

Assess Space and Layout: Begin by evaluating the available space in your vehicle. Consider the dimensions, layout, and any existing compartments that can be utilized.

Equipment Placement: Strategically position your equipment based on frequency of use and accessibility. Place frequently used tools within easy reach, while storing less commonly used items in secure compartments.

Shelving and Racks: Install shelving units or racks to create designated storage areas for tools, cleaning products, and supplies. Adjustable shelves allow you to accommodate varying equipment sizes.

Storage Compartments: Utilize storage compartments, drawers, and bins to keep small items organized. Label compartments for quick identification and retrieval.

Tool Holders: Install holders, clips, or hooks for hanging tools like brushes, towels, and extension cords. This prevents clutter and keeps items off the floor.

Secure Equipment: Use straps, bungee cords, or fasteners to secure equipment during transit. Prevent shifting and potential damage while driving.

Water Tanks and Hoses: Install water tanks securely and ensure hoses are neatly coiled to prevent tangling. Plan for spill containment in case of leaks.

Chemical Storage: Store cleaning chemicals upright to prevent leaks. Use spill-proof containers or trays to contain any accidental spills.

Work Surfaces: Create dedicated work surfaces for tasks like mixing cleaning solutions, prepping equipment, and detailing. Foldable tables or countertops can be useful.

Cabin Organization: Keep the cabin organized and clutter-free. Use storage solutions for personal items like snacks, drinks, and documentation.

Safety Equipment: Allocate space for safety equipment like a first aid kit, fire extinguisher, and personal protective gear. Ensure these items are easily accessible.

Waste Management: Integrate a waste management system within your vehicle, including trash bags and containers for disposing of used cleaning materials.

Lighting: Install adequate lighting in your workspace area to ensure visibility during detailing tasks, especially in low-light conditions.

Electrical Outlets: If using electrical equipment, ensure easy access to power outlets. Use extension cords and surge protectors to safely power your tools.

Labeling and Color Coding: Use labels and color coding to identify different equipment, cleaning products, and tools. This simplifies retrieval and minimizes confusion.

Regular Maintenance: Dedicate time to cleaning and organizing your workspace after each job. This ensures that everything remains in order and ready for the next task.

Flexibility and Adaptability: Design your workspace with adaptability in mind. As your business grows or your services evolve, your workspace layout should accommodate changes.

By following these steps, you can create an efficient, organized, and safe workspace within your mobile car detailing vehicle. An optimized workspace enhances your operational efficiency, allows you to focus on delivering quality services, and leaves a positive impression on your clients.

Equipping Your Vehicle With Water And Power Supply Systems

Equipping your mobile car detailing vehicle with water and power supply systems is essential for delivering quality services on the go. Here's a comprehensive guide to help you set up these systems effectively:

Water Supply System:

Water Tanks: Choose appropriate water tanks based on your business needs. Consider portable tanks with secure fittings and capacities that suit the size of your vehicle.

Water Source: Determine whether you'll fill up water tanks at a central location or have an arrangement with clients for water hookup.

Pumps and Hoses: Install a water pump to facilitate efficient water flow. Attach high-quality hoses with connectors to ensure a secure water supply.

Gravity Feed Option: If your vehicle has limited space, consider a gravity feed setup. Elevate water tanks to create pressure for water flow without a pump.

Filtration System: Incorporate a filtration system to ensure that the water you use is clean and free from contaminants. This prevents damage to vehicle surfaces during washing.

Pressure Regulator: Install a pressure regulator to control water pressure. This prevents excessive water usage and damage to delicate surfaces.

Quick-Connect Fittings: Use quick-connect fittings for hoses and water supply components. These make setup and disassembly more efficient.

Spill Containment: Plan for spill containment solutions in case of water leaks or spills. This prevents environmental damage.

Power Supply System:

Generator: Choose a portable generator with sufficient wattage to power your equipment. Consider factors like the power requirements of your pressure washer, vacuum, and other tools.

Inverter: Install a power inverter to convert DC power from your vehicle's battery to AC power for operating electrical equipment.

Electrical Outlets: Position electrical outlets strategically within your vehicle for easy access. Use surge protectors to safeguard your equipment.

Extension Cords: Have a supply of heavy-duty extension cords that reach various areas around your workspace.

Battery Bank: Consider a battery bank as an alternative power source. This can be charged when your vehicle is running and provide power for short tasks.

Wiring and Safety: Ensure proper wiring to avoid electrical hazards. Use waterproof connections and circuit breakers for safety.

Equipment Compatibility: Confirm that your equipment can operate on the generator's power output. Some sensitive tools might require a pure sine wave inverter.

Maintenance and Fuel: Regularly maintain your generator, check oil levels, and keep it fueled to ensure uninterrupted power supply during detailing sessions.

Integrated Setup:

Space Optimization: Design your vehicle's interior layout to accommodate water tanks, generators, and equipment securely while ensuring easy access.

Secure Mounting: Install tanks, generators, and equipment securely to prevent shifting during transit. Use brackets, straps, and fasteners as needed.

Ventilation: Ensure proper ventilation for your generator to prevent overheating. Position it in a well-ventilated area to dissipate heat effectively.

Safety Precautions: Follow safety guidelines for handling water tanks, generators, and electrical components. Install safety features like gas detectors and fire extinguishers.

Regular Checks: Perform regular checks on your water and power supply systems to identify and address any issues promptly.

By following these steps, you can equip your mobile car detailing vehicle with reliable water and power supply systems. These setups ensure that you can deliver professional detailing services efficiently and without interruptions, enhancing the customer experience and the success of your business.

Safety Measures For Transporting Equipment And Chemicals

Ensuring safety when transporting equipment and chemicals for your mobile car detailing business is paramount. Here's a comprehensive guide to help you implement necessary safety measures:

Equipment Transport Safety:

Secure Mounting: Securely fasten all equipment, tools, and containers within your vehicle to prevent movement during transit. Use brackets, straps, and bungee cords as needed.

Compartment Organization: Organize your vehicle's interior with designated compartments, shelves, and racks for different equipment. This prevents items from shifting and causing hazards.

Weight Distribution: Distribute weight evenly within your vehicle to maintain stability and prevent overloading. Avoid putting excessive weight on one side.

Padding and Cushioning: Use padding, foam, or blankets to cushion equipment and prevent damage during transit. This is especially important for fragile items.

Secure Lids and Covers: Ensure that containers and lids are tightly secured to prevent spills and leaks. Use locking mechanisms if available.

Chemical Separation: Store chemicals away from sensitive equipment and tools to avoid accidental mixing or contamination.

Emergency Supplies: Keep a spill cleanup kit, absorbent materials, and personal protective equipment (PPE) within reach in case of spills or accidents.

Chemical Transport Safety:

Proper Containers: Use leak-proof, chemical-resistant containers for storing and transporting chemicals. Ensure containers are properly labeled with contents and warnings.

Storage Compatibility: Store chemicals in a way that prevents interactions and reactions between different substances. Follow manufacturer guidelines.

Ventilation: Transport chemicals in a well-ventilated area to prevent the buildup of fumes and odors. Avoid transporting chemicals in the passenger compartment.

Separation: Keep chemicals separate from tools, equipment, and personal items to prevent cross-contamination.

Spill Containment: Use spill-proof trays, containers, or barriers to contain potential spills and leaks. This prevents chemicals from spreading within your vehicle.

Emergency Information: Carry Material Safety Data Sheets (MSDS) or Safety Data Sheets (SDS) for each chemical you transport. These sheets provide crucial information in case of accidents.

Personal Protection: Wear appropriate personal protective equipment (PPE) such as gloves, safety glasses, and aprons when handling and transporting chemicals.

Storage During Transit: Position chemical containers upright and ensure they are stable during transit. Secure them to prevent tipping or movement.

Vehicle Safety:

Vehicle Maintenance: Regularly maintain your vehicle to ensure it's in optimal condition for safe transportation. Check tires, brakes, and suspension systems.

Safe Driving Practices: Adhere to safe driving practices, obey traffic laws, and avoid distractions while on the road.

Emergency Equipment: Carry emergency equipment such as a first aid kit, fire extinguisher, and roadside safety gear.

Regular Inspections: Conduct regular inspections of your vehicle, equipment, and chemical containers to identify any issues that might compromise safety.

By implementing these safety measures, you can ensure the safe transportation of equipment and chemicals for your mobile car detailing business. Prioritizing safety not only protects you and your clients but also enhances your professionalism and reputation.

* * *

CHAPTER 6: DEVELOPING SERVICE PACKAGES

Creating A Range Of Detailing Packages To Cater To Different Customer Needs

Creating a range of detailing packages tailored to different customers' needs is a strategic approach that enhances your mobile car detailing business. Here's a step-by-step guide to help you design diverse and appealing detailing packages:

1. Customer Segmentation:
Identify different customer segments based on factors like budget, vehicle type, preferences, and detailing needs. Segmentation allows you to offer packages that cater to specific groups.

2. Service Customization:
Offer a mix of basic and advanced services within your packages. Allow customers to customize packages by choosing additional services or upgrades.

3. Package Tier Structure:
Create a tiered structure with packages that gradually offer more comprehensive services. This enables customers to choose the level of detailing they prefer.

4. Core Services:
Each package should include a set of core services such as exterior wash, interior vacuuming, window cleaning, and tire dressing. These are essential

in all packages.

5. Additional Services:
Add specialized services to higher-tier packages, such as paint correction, waxing, leather conditioning, engine bay cleaning, or headlight restoration.

6. Bundle Savings:
Offer cost savings for customers who opt for higher-tier packages. Clearly communicate the value they receive by upgrading to a more comprehensive package.

7. Pricing Strategy:
Set competitive and reasonable prices for each package based on the services offered, market rates, and your business expenses.

8. Transparent Descriptions:
Provide clear and concise descriptions of what each package includes. Avoid technical jargon and use customer-friendly language.

9. Visual Representation:
Use visual aids such as images, diagrams, or videos to illustrate the differences between packages and showcase the outcomes of each service.

10. Upselling Opportunities:
Include options for customers to add individual services to their chosen package, encouraging upselling and maximizing revenue per customer.

11. Seasonal or Special Packages:
Create limited-time packages tied to specific seasons or events. For example, offer "Spring Cleaning" or "Holiday Special" packages with unique services.

12. Subscription Models:
Introduce subscription-based packages where customers can opt for monthly or quarterly detailing services at a discounted rate.

13. Customer Feedback:

Gather feedback from existing customers to understand their preferences and pain points. Use this input to refine and create packages that resonate with your target audience.

14. Simplicity and Clarity:
Keep package names and descriptions simple and easy to understand. Customers should quickly grasp what each package entails.

15. Test and Adjust:
Launch your packages and monitor customer response. Analyze which packages are popular and which might need adjustments based on customer feedback.

16. Ongoing Optimization:
Regularly review and update your detailing packages to align with changing customer demands, industry trends, and your business's growth.

By following these steps, you can create a range of detailing packages that cater to a variety of customers' needs and preferences. Offering diverse options enhances customer satisfaction, encourages repeat business, and positions your mobile car detailing business as a trusted choice in the market.

Pricing Strategies And Competitive Analysis

Developing effective pricing strategies and conducting competitive analysis are essential steps for the success of your mobile car detailing business. Here's a guide to help you with these aspects:

Pricing Strategies:

Cost-Based Pricing: Calculate your costs, including equipment, supplies, labor, and overhead. Add a desired profit margin to determine your pricing. This approach ensures you cover expenses and generate profit.

Value-Based Pricing: Consider the value your detailing services bring to customers. Set prices based on the benefits customers receive, such as improved vehicle appearance, convenience, and time savings.

Competitive Pricing: Research your competitors' pricing to ensure your rates are competitive within your local market. Price your services in a way that reflects your quality and offerings.

Dynamic Pricing: Adjust your prices based on factors like demand, seasonality, and special events. For example, you might charge more during busy periods or offer discounts during slow months.

Bundle Pricing: Offer discounted rates for bundled packages. Encourage customers to choose higher-tier packages by showcasing the cost savings of bundling services.

Penetration Pricing: Initially offer lower prices to attract new customers and build a client base. Once established, you can gradually increase prices based on demand and reputation.

Premium Pricing: If you position your business as offering high-quality, premium detailing services, set higher prices that reflect the exclusivity and superior results.

Competitive Analysis:

Identify Competitors: Identify direct and indirect competitors in your local area. These could include other mobile detailers, car washes, and detailing shops.

Analyze Pricing: Research the pricing structures of your competitors. Compare the range of services they offer and the corresponding prices.

Service Comparison: Compare the services included in your packages with those offered by competitors. Highlight any unique or additional services you provide.

Quality Assessment: Assess the quality of work offered by competitors. If your services are superior, you can justify higher pricing.

Customer Reviews: Study online reviews and customer feedback about your competitors. This can provide insights into their strengths and weaknesses.

Market Positioning: Determine where your business fits in terms of quality and pricing compared to competitors. Decide whether you want to position yourself as a premium, mid-range, or budget option.

Unique Selling Proposition (USP): Identify what sets your mobile detailing business apart from competitors. This could be exceptional customer service, specialized services, or eco-friendly practices.

Value-Added Services: Offer value-added services that competitors don't provide. This justifies higher pricing and attracts customers seeking a more comprehensive experience.

Pricing Flexibility: Be prepared to adjust your prices based on the competitive landscape and customer preferences. However, avoid underpricing to maintain profitability.

Customer Perception: Understand how customers perceive your competitors' pricing and your own. Pricing should align with the value customers perceive in your services.

By implementing these pricing strategies and conducting a thorough competitive analysis, you can establish pricing that is both competitive and reflective of the value you offer. Continuously monitor the market, gather customer feedback, and refine your pricing strategy to stay competitive and profitable in the mobile car detailing industry.

Upselling And Cross-Selling Techniques To Maximize Revenue

Implementing effective upselling and cross-selling techniques can significantly boost revenue for your mobile car detailing business. Here's a guide to help you make the most of these strategies:

Upselling Techniques:

Bundle Upgrades: Offer customers the option to upgrade their detailing package with additional services at a discounted rate. For example, offer a discounted interior detailing upgrade when they book an exterior wash.

Premium Packages: Present premium packages with enhanced services such as paint correction, ceramic coating, or specialized treatments. Highlight the superior results and protection they provide.

Service Enhancements: Suggest service enhancements like upgraded wax or sealant options, premium tire dressing, or headlight restoration.

Loyalty Programs: Create loyalty programs where repeat customers receive exclusive benefits or discounts on their next detailing service.

Seasonal Promotions: Introduce seasonal promotions that encourage customers to try higher-tier packages with discounts or added services during specific times of the year.

Personalized Recommendations: Tailor your upselling efforts based on the customer's vehicle type, condition, and specific needs. Personalization enhances the value proposition.

Cross-Selling Techniques:

Complementary Services: Recommend complementary services that naturally align with the customer's chosen package. For instance, when booking interior detailing, suggest adding upholstery protection.

Interior-Exterior Combo: Offer discounted rates when customers choose both interior and exterior detailing services together. Emphasize the comprehensive transformation of the entire vehicle.

Maintenance Packages: Introduce maintenance packages that include regular touch-up services at a reduced rate for customers who want to maintain the appearance of their vehicle over time.

Add-On Products: Promote additional products such as air fresheners, microfiber towels, or interior cleaning kits. Offer these products as convenient add-ons during the booking process.

Package Combos: Create package combinations that cover a range of detailing needs. For example, offer a "Complete Overhaul" package that includes paint correction, interior detailing, and protection services.

Gift Certificates: Encourage customers to purchase gift certificates for friends or family members, promoting your services and potentially bringing in new customers.

Additional Techniques:

Educational Content: Provide educational content through your website, blog, or social media about the benefits of various detailing services. This can prompt customers to inquire about additional services.

Visual Aids: Use before-and-after photos or videos to showcase the transformative results of upsell and cross-sell services.

Clear Communication: Clearly communicate the value and benefits of each upsell and cross-sell option. Customers should understand how these services enhance their vehicle's appearance and protection.

Training Staff: If you have employees, train them to recommend upsells and cross-sells based on customer interactions and vehicle assessment.

Post-Service Suggestions: After completing a detailing service, provide customers with recommendations for maintaining the vehicle's appearance and suggest future services.

By incorporating these upselling and cross-selling techniques, you can effectively increase revenue while enhancing the customer experience. Tailor your approach based on customer preferences and vehicle conditions to maximize the success of these strategies in your mobile car detailing business.

CHAPTER 7: MARKETING AND BRANDING

Building A Strong Brand Identity For Your Mobile Detailing Business

Building a strong brand identity is crucial for establishing a distinct presence and reputation for your mobile car detailing business. Here's a step-by-step approach to help you create a compelling brand identity:

1. Define Your Brand Identity:

Mission and Values: Clearly define your business's mission, values, and core principles. Identify what sets your mobile detailing business apart from competitors.

Target Audience: Understand your target customers' demographics, preferences, and pain points. Tailor your brand identity to resonate with their needs.

2. Brand Name and Logo:

Choose a Memorable Name: Select a name that's easy to remember and reflects the essence of your services.

Design a Unique Logo: Create a professional logo that visually represents your brand. The logo should be simple, scalable, and recognizable.

3. Brand Visuals:

Color Palette: Choose a consistent color palette that resonates with your business values and appeals to your target audience.

Typography: Select fonts that are easy to read and reflect the tone of your brand, whether it's professional, modern, or approachable.

Imagery: Use high-quality images that showcase your detailing work, vehicles, and satisfied customers. Consistent imagery reinforces your brand identity.

4. Brand Messaging:

Tagline: Craft a memorable tagline that encapsulates your brand's promise and value proposition.

Voice and Tone: Define your brand's voice and tone. Whether it's friendly, authoritative, or informative, maintain consistency across all communications.

Key Messages: Develop key messages that communicate the benefits of your services and what customers can expect.

5. Online Presence:

Website: Create a professional and user-friendly website that showcases your services, portfolio, pricing, and contact information.

Social Media Profiles: Set up active social media profiles on platforms where your target audience is present. Regularly post engaging content related to car care and detailing.

6. Consistent Branding:

Use Across Channels: Apply your brand identity consistently across all platforms, from your website and social media to business cards and promotional materials.

Vehicle Branding: If applicable, brand your mobile detailing vehicle with your logo, name, and contact information.

7. Customer Experience:

Consistency: Ensure the experience customers receive matches your brand promise, from the quality of your services to your interactions.

Personalization: Provide a personalized experience that reflects your brand's values and establishes a strong emotional connection with customers.

8. Customer Feedback:

Listen and Adapt: Pay attention to customer feedback and adjust your brand identity based on their preferences and suggestions.
9. Partnerships and Collaborations:

Partnerships: Collaborate with local automotive businesses or events to increase your brand visibility and establish credibility.
10. Long-Term Brand Building:

Consistency and Persistence: Building a strong brand identity takes time. Continuously uphold your brand values, visuals, and messaging to reinforce your identity.
By following these steps, you can build a strong and memorable brand identity for your mobile detailing business. A well-defined brand identity helps you stand out in the market, attract loyal customers, and create a lasting impression that drives business growth.

Creating A Professional And User-Friendly Website And Social Media Profiles

Creating a professional and user-friendly website and social media profile is essential for establishing a strong online presence for your mobile car detailing business. Here's a guide to help you achieve this:

Creating a Professional Website:

Choose a Domain and Hosting:
Register a domain name that reflects your business. Choose a reliable web hosting service to ensure your website is accessible and loads quickly.

Clear Navigation:
Design a user-friendly navigation menu that allows visitors to easily find information about your services, pricing, contact details, and portfolio.

Responsive Design:
Create a responsive website that adapts to different screen sizes, ensuring a seamless experience for users on desktops, tablets, and smartphones.

High-Quality Imagery:
Showcase your detailing work with high-quality images that highlight the transformation your services provide. Include before-and-after photos.

Service Descriptions:
Clearly describe your detailing packages, highlighting the benefits and unique features of each service. Use customer-friendly language.

Pricing Information:
Provide transparent pricing details for each package. If needed, offer a "Get a Quote" option for personalized service estimates.

Contact Information:
Place your contact details prominently on every page. Include a contact form for inquiries and a map if you have a physical location.

Testimonials and Reviews:
Display customer testimonials and reviews to build trust and showcase the positive experiences your clients have had.

About Us Page:

Share a brief history of your business, your values, and your passion for car detailing. This helps establish a personal connection with visitors.

Call-to-Action Buttons:
Use clear call-to-action buttons that direct visitors to book services, request a quote, or contact you. These encourage user interaction.

Blog or Resources:
If possible, maintain a blog or resources section with informative articles about car care, detailing tips, and industry trends. This establishes you as an expert.

Creating Professional Social Media Profiles:

Choose the Right Platforms:
Select social media platforms that align with your target audience. Common platforms for car-related businesses include Instagram, Facebook, and Pinterest.

Consistent Branding:
Use your logo, brand colors, and imagery consistently across all social media profiles. This ensures brand recognition.

Engaging Content:
Post engaging content related to car care, detailing tips, industry news, and behind-the-scenes glimpses of your work.

Visual Content:
Share high-quality images and videos that showcase your detailing work, vehicles, and satisfied customers. Visual content is essential for your industry.

Regular Updates:
Maintain an active presence by posting regularly. Consistency is key to keeping your audience engaged.

Engage with Followers:

Respond promptly to comments, messages, and inquiries. Engage with your followers by answering their questions and fostering conversations.

Promotions and Giveaways:
Offer promotions, discounts, and occasional giveaways to encourage user engagement and attract new followers.

Links to Website:
Include links to your website and specific service pages in your social media profiles. Make it easy for users to access more information.

By following these guidelines, you can create a professional and user-friendly website and social media profiles for your mobile car detailing business. A strong online presence enhances your credibility, attracts customers, and establishes a positive brand image in the competitive automotive industry.

Implementing Effective Marketing Strategies, Including Online And Offline Approaches

Implementing effective marketing strategies, both online and offline, is crucial for promoting your mobile car detailing business and attracting customers. Here's a comprehensive guide to help you navigate these strategies:

Online Marketing Strategies:

Professional Website:
Build a user-friendly website that showcases your services, pricing, portfolio, and contact information. Optimize it for search engines to improve online visibility.

Search Engine Optimization (SEO):
Optimize your website with relevant keywords, meta tags, and quality content to rank higher on search engine results pages. This increases

organic traffic.

Local Business Listings:
Create and claim your business listings on platforms like Google My Business, Yelp, and other local directories. Provide accurate and consistent information.

Social Media Marketing:
Establish active profiles on social media platforms relevant to your audience. Share engaging content, images, videos, and interact with followers.

Content Marketing:
Maintain a blog on your website with informative articles about car care, detailing tips, and industry insights. This positions you as an authority in your field.

Email Marketing:
Collect customer emails and send regular newsletters with promotions, tips, and updates. Email marketing keeps your audience engaged and informed.

Online Advertising:
Invest in pay-per-click (PPC) advertising on platforms like Google Ads and social media. Target specific keywords and demographics to reach potential customers.

Social Media Advertising:
Utilize paid social media ads to reach a broader audience and target users based on location, interests, and behaviors.

Online Reviews and Testimonials:
Encourage satisfied customers to leave positive reviews on platforms like Google and Yelp. Respond to reviews, both positive and negative, to demonstrate your commitment to customer satisfaction.

Visual Content:

Share high-quality images and videos showcasing your detailing work. Visual content is powerful for demonstrating the quality of your services.

Offline Marketing Strategies:

Networking:
Attend local automotive events, car shows, and business networking events to connect with potential customers and industry professionals.

Local Partnerships:
Collaborate with local auto shops, dealerships, or car rental companies for cross-promotions and referrals.

Flyers and Brochures:
Design and distribute printed materials with information about your services and contact details. Place them at local businesses, community centers, and car-related events.

Vehicle Branding:
Brand your mobile detailing vehicle with your logo, contact information, and a brief description of your services. It's a moving advertisement.

Direct Mail:
Send targeted direct mail to local households or businesses to introduce your services. Offer exclusive discounts or promotions to encourage response.

Community Involvement:
Sponsor local events, sports teams, or charity initiatives. Community involvement enhances your brand's reputation and visibility.

Referral Program:
Implement a referral program where existing customers receive rewards or discounts for referring new clients to your services.

Branded Merchandise:

Create branded merchandise like T-shirts, hats, or car accessories. Offer these as giveaways or sell them to customers.

By combining these online and offline marketing strategies, you can effectively promote your mobile car detailing business, increase visibility, and attract a steady stream of customers. Remember to track the effectiveness of each strategy and adjust your approach based on results and customer feedback.

* * *

CHAPTER 8: CUSTOMER ACQUISITION AND RETENTION

Strategies For Attracting Your First Customers And Building A Client Base

When starting a mobile car detailing business, a combination of online and local strategies can help you attract your first customers and build a solid client base:

1. Local Networking and Partnerships:
Attend local automotive events, car shows, and community gatherings to introduce yourself to potential customers. Forge partnerships with local auto shops, dealerships, and car clubs to gain referrals and establish credibility within the community.

2. Word-of-Mouth and Referrals:
Leverage your personal network and encourage friends, family, and acquaintances to spread the word about your new business. Offering an incentive for referrals can motivate them to refer customers to you.

3. Local Online Listings:
Claim and optimize your business listings on platforms like Google My Business and Yelp. These listings help you appear in local search results when people are looking for car detailing services in your area.

4. Social Media Engagement:
Establish a strong presence on social media platforms that resonate with your target audience. Share high-quality images of your work, engage with followers, and respond promptly to inquiries and comments.

5. Limited-Time Promotions:
Offer special promotions or discounts for your initial customers as a way to incentivize them to give your services a try. This can create initial buzz and encourage people to book appointments.

6. Flyers and Local Advertising:
Create eye-catching flyers and distribute them in local businesses, community centers, and places where car enthusiasts frequent. Local newspapers and magazines can also be effective for targeted advertising.

7. Door-to-Door Outreach:
Visit local neighborhoods and offer your services door-to-door. This personal approach can help you connect directly with potential customers.

8. Personalized Direct Mail:
Send personalized direct mail to nearby households introducing your services, along with an exclusive offer for new clients.

9. Online Portfolio and Testimonials:
Build an impressive online portfolio showcasing your before-and-after work on different vehicles. Display customer testimonials and reviews to establish trust and credibility.

10. Launch Event:
Organize a launch event or open house where you can demonstrate your services, offer free car inspections, and provide special discounts for attendees.

11. Online Advertising:
Utilize targeted online advertising on platforms like Google Ads and social media to reach local customers actively looking for car detailing services.

12. Engaging Content:
Regularly share engaging content related to car care, detailing tips, and industry insights on your website and social media. Establish yourself as a knowledgeable expert.

Combining these strategies allows you to create a comprehensive approach to attract your first customers and start building a strong client base. As you gain experience and positive customer feedback, your reputation will grow, and word-of-mouth recommendations will contribute to the ongoing growth of your mobile car detailing business.

Providing Exceptional Customer Service To Enhance Retention

Delivering exceptional customer service is essential for retaining clients and fostering loyalty in your mobile car detailing business. Here's a guide to help you provide outstanding service:

1. Professionalism:
Approach every interaction with professionalism. Be punctual, well-groomed, and courteous when communicating with clients.

2. Clear Communication:
Maintain open and transparent communication. Clearly explain your services, pricing, and any potential delays.

3. Personalization:
Tailor your services to each client's specific needs. Take note of their preferences and any special requests.

4. Active Listening:
Listen attentively to your clients. Ask questions to understand their expectations and address any concerns they may have.

5. Quality Work:

Deliver consistently high-quality detailing services. Pay attention to detail and ensure your work exceeds client expectations.

6. Time Management:
Respect your clients' time by sticking to agreed-upon schedules. If delays are inevitable, communicate promptly and apologize for any inconvenience.

7. Convenience:
Offer mobile services that provide convenience to clients by detailing their vehicles at their preferred location.

8. Educate Clients:
Educate clients about proper car care between detailing sessions. Share tips on maintaining their vehicle's appearance.

9. Follow-Up:
Reach out to clients after the service to ensure their satisfaction. Address any concerns and express your willingness to make improvements.

10. Loyalty Programs:
Introduce loyalty programs that reward repeat customers with special discounts, promotions, or exclusive services.

11. Personal Touches:
Add personal touches such as a thank-you note or a small gift after completing a detailing service.

12. Problem Resolution:
Handle complaints or issues with empathy and a willingness to resolve them quickly and effectively.

13. Consistency:
Strive for consistency in the quality of your services, communication, and overall customer experience.

14. Surveys and Feedback:

Gather feedback through surveys or reviews to identify areas for improvement and showcase your commitment to enhancing customer satisfaction.

15. Continuous Improvement:
Regularly assess and refine your customer service processes based on feedback and changing customer needs.

16. Empower Your Team:
If you have employees, ensure they understand the importance of exceptional customer service and provide them with the necessary training and resources.

17. Appreciation:
Express gratitude to your clients for choosing your services and for their continued support.

By focusing on these customer service practices, you'll create a positive and memorable experience for your clients. Exceptional customer service not only enhances client retention but also leads to positive word-of-mouth recommendations, referrals, and the long-term success of your mobile car detailing business.

Collecting And Utilizing Customer Feedback To Improve Your Services

Collecting and utilizing customer feedback is a valuable way to enhance your mobile car detailing services. Here's a step-by-step approach to effectively gather and apply customer feedback:

1. Choose Feedback Channels:
Determine the channels through which you'll collect feedback, such as email surveys, online reviews, social media, or feedback forms on your website.

2. Timing Matters:
Request feedback shortly after providing a detailing service while the experience is fresh in your customers' minds.

3. Use Open-Ended Questions:
Frame questions in a way that encourages detailed responses. Ask about their overall experience, satisfaction, and areas for improvement.

4. Offer Multiple Options:
Provide a mix of multiple-choice questions and open-ended questions to gather quantitative and qualitative feedback.

5. Listen Actively:
Carefully review and analyze the feedback you receive. Pay attention to recurring themes and specific suggestions.

6. Positive Reinforcement:
Acknowledge and appreciate positive feedback from customers. This can encourage more customers to share their experiences.

7. Address Negative Feedback:
Respond promptly and professionally to negative feedback. Apologize if necessary and outline steps you'll take to address the issue.

8. Implement Changes:
Use feedback to identify areas for improvement in your services, processes, or customer interactions.

9. Continuous Training:
If you have employees, use feedback to identify training needs and opportunities for improving their skills and interactions.

10. Focus on Key Areas:
Prioritize feedback related to critical aspects of your service, such as quality of work, communication, and punctuality.

11. Share Improvements:

Communicate changes and improvements to your customers. Show that their feedback is valued and leads to positive changes.

12. Measure Over Time:
Monitor feedback trends over time to evaluate the impact of changes and ensure consistent improvement.

13. Encourage Ongoing Feedback:
Keep the feedback loop open by encouraging customers to share their thoughts and suggestions regularly.

14. Reward Participation:
Consider offering incentives or discounts to customers who provide feedback. This encourages more people to engage.

15. Test New Ideas:
Use feedback to test new services or offerings. Gauge customer interest before making significant changes.

16. Celebrate Successes:
Highlight instances where customer feedback led to positive changes. This reinforces your commitment to continuous improvement.

By systematically collecting and applying customer feedback, you can refine your mobile car detailing services, address areas for improvement, and create a client-centered approach. This not only enhances customer satisfaction but also strengthens your reputation and contributes to the long-term success of your business.

* * *

CHAPTER 9: OPERATIONAL EFFICIENCY AND TIME MANAGEMENT

Optimizing Your Workflow To Handle Appointments Effectively

Optimizing your workflow is essential to efficiently manage appointments and provide excellent service in your mobile car detailing business. Here's a step-by-step approach to enhance your appointment handling process:

1. Online Booking System:
Implement an online booking system on your website. This allows customers to schedule appointments at their convenience, reducing back-and-forth communication.

2. Calendar Management:
Use a digital calendar or scheduling software to keep track of appointments, set availability, and avoid overbooking.

3. Define Service Zones:
Divide your service area into zones and assign specific days or times for each zone. This minimizes travel time between appointments.

4. Buffer Time:

Incorporate buffer time between appointments to account for unexpected delays and ensure you have enough time to complete each service thoroughly.

5. Confirmation and Reminders:
Send automated confirmation emails or messages to clients upon booking. Send reminders closer to the appointment date to minimize no-shows.

6. Pre-Appointment Communication:
Prior to the appointment, communicate expectations, such as access to water and power sources, and any preparation required from the customer.

7. Efficient Route Planning:
Plan your appointments geographically to minimize travel time between locations. Use navigation apps to find the quickest routes.

8. Organized Equipment:
Keep your detailing equipment organized and easily accessible in your mobile vehicle. This ensures a smoother setup and cleanup process.

9. Streamlined Set-Up:
Develop a standardized set-up process for your detailing equipment to minimize the time it takes to start each appointment.

10. Mobile Payments:
Offer mobile payment options to facilitate quick and secure transactions at the end of each service.

11. Customer Records:
Maintain a customer database with their service history and preferences. Personalize interactions based on their past experiences.

12. Upsell Opportunities:
Train your team, if applicable, to identify upselling opportunities during appointments without causing disruptions.

13. Post-Service Feedback:

Gather feedback immediately after the service to ensure customer satisfaction and address any concerns promptly.

14. Regular Evaluations:
Periodically review your workflow to identify bottlenecks or areas for improvement. Adjust your processes based on your findings.

15. Employee Training:
If you have employees, provide thorough training on your optimized workflow to ensure consistency and efficiency.

16. Technology Integration:
Explore mobile apps and tools that can help streamline your workflow, from appointment scheduling to navigation.

By following these steps, you can create a well-organized and efficient workflow that enables you to handle appointments effectively, enhance customer satisfaction, and maximize the productivity of your mobile car detailing business.

Scheduling And Route Planning For Maximum Efficiency

Scheduling and route planning are critical components of ensuring maximum efficiency in your mobile car detailing business. Here's a practical guide to help you manage appointments and plan routes effectively:

1. Online Booking System:
Implement an online booking system that allows customers to choose available time slots. This reduces scheduling conflicts and eliminates the need for manual coordination.

2. Define Service Zones:
Divide your service area into zones based on location. Assign specific days or time slots for each zone to minimize travel distances between

appointments.

3. Centralized Scheduling:
Use scheduling software or a digital calendar to manage appointments in one centralized location. This avoids double-bookings and keeps you organized.

4. Prioritize Proximity:
When scheduling, prioritize appointments that are geographically close to each other. This minimizes travel time and maximizes efficiency.

5. Time Blocks:
Group appointments within specific time blocks. This allows you to focus on similar services consecutively, reducing setup and transition times.

6. Buffer Time:
Allocate buffer time between appointments to account for traffic, unexpected delays, and thorough cleanup. This prevents rushing between jobs.

7. Route Planning Apps:
Utilize navigation apps with route optimization features. Input all your appointments to find the most efficient route that saves time and fuel.

8. Real-Time Traffic Updates:
Monitor traffic conditions using apps or GPS devices that offer real-time updates. Adjust your routes accordingly to avoid delays.

9. Strategic Start and End Points:
Plan your day's route to start and end in areas that minimize commuting time from your home or central location.

10. Flexibility for Additions:
Keep a portion of your schedule open for last-minute appointments or emergency services. Flexibility can accommodate new clients without disrupting your overall plan.

11. Efficient Equipment Setup:
Organize your detailing equipment in your mobile vehicle to optimize setup and breakdown times at each location.

12. Reconfirm Appointments:
Send reminders to clients the day before or the morning of the appointment. This helps reduce no-shows and ensures they're prepared.

13. Regular Route Review:
Periodically review your route planning strategy to identify potential optimizations based on patterns and changes in your service area.

14. Continuous Monitoring:
Throughout the day, monitor your route and adjust for unexpected traffic or changes in appointment timing.

15. Regular Evaluations:
Evaluate the efficiency of your scheduling and route planning approach. Make adjustments as needed based on feedback and lessons learned.

By following these guidelines, you can streamline your scheduling and route planning processes to achieve maximum efficiency in your mobile car detailing business. Effective scheduling and route planning not only save time and resources but also contribute to a smoother and more satisfying experience for both you and your customers.

Hiring And Training Staff, If Necessary, To Scale Your Business

Hiring and training staff is a strategic step to scale your mobile car detailing business. Here's a comprehensive guide to help you effectively recruit and train your team:

1. Define Roles and Responsibilities:
Clearly outline the roles you need to fill, such as detailers, customer service, or administrative positions. Define the responsibilities associated with each

role.

2. Create Job Descriptions:
Develop detailed job descriptions that outline key responsibilities, required skills, qualifications, and expectations for each role.

3. Recruitment Strategy:
Use a combination of job boards, social media, local community networks, and referrals to attract potential candidates.

4. Interview Process:
Conduct structured interviews to assess candidates' skills, experience, and cultural fit with your business. Ask behavioral and situational questions to gauge their suitability.

5. Training Plan:
Develop a comprehensive training program that covers technical skills, customer service, safety protocols, and adherence to your brand standards.

6. Onboarding Process:
Create an onboarding process that introduces new hires to your business values, procedures, and company culture. Provide an overview of their role's importance in the overall business.

7. Technical Training:
Train detailers in proper cleaning techniques, equipment operation, and the use of detailing products to ensure consistent service quality.

8. Customer Interaction Training:
Train customer-facing staff in effective communication, conflict resolution, and delivering exceptional customer experiences.

9. Safety and Environmental Training:
Educate your team on safety measures, proper handling of chemicals, and adherence to environmental regulations during detailing operations.

10. Quality Control:

Establish quality control standards and procedures to ensure that all team members consistently deliver high-quality services.

11. Soft Skills Development:
Emphasize soft skills like punctuality, professionalism, and teamwork. These skills contribute to a positive work environment and customer satisfaction.

12. Continuous Learning:
Encourage ongoing learning and improvement by offering opportunities for skill development, attending workshops, and staying updated on industry trends.

13. Supervision and Feedback:
Assign experienced team members to mentor and supervise new hires. Provide regular feedback to help them improve and grow.

14. Team Collaboration:
Foster a collaborative environment where team members share knowledge, experiences, and best practices to enhance overall performance.

15. Performance Evaluation:
Establish a performance evaluation system to assess employees' progress and identify areas for improvement or additional training.

16. Incentives and Recognition:
Implement an incentive program or recognition system that rewards exceptional performance and encourages motivation.

17. Adaptability:
As your business grows, remain flexible in adjusting your training programs to accommodate new roles and evolving responsibilities.

By following these steps, you can effectively hire and train staff to help scale your mobile car detailing business. A well-trained and motivated team contributes to consistent service quality, enhanced customer satisfaction, and the successful expansion of your business.

* * *

CHAPTER 10: SCALING AND FUTURE GROWTH

Evaluating The Potential For Expansion And Additional Service Offerings

Evaluating the potential for expansion and additional service offerings in your mobile car detailing business requires careful consideration and strategic planning. Here's a step-by-step approach to help you assess these opportunities:

1. Market Research:
Conduct thorough market research to understand current industry trends, customer demands, and competitive landscape. Identify any gaps or opportunities that align with your business's strengths.

2. Customer Feedback:
Gather feedback from your existing customers to gauge their interest in potential expansion or additional services. Their insights can provide valuable insights into untapped areas.

3. Competitor Analysis:
Analyze what services your competitors are offering and identify areas where you can differentiate yourself or provide superior offerings.

4. Industry Trends:
Stay updated on emerging trends in the car detailing and automotive industry. This can help you anticipate future demand for new services.

5. Financial Analysis:
Evaluate the financial feasibility of expanding or adding new services. Consider the costs associated with equipment, training, marketing, and potential revenue generation.

6. Resource Availability:
Assess your current resources, including equipment, staff, and operational capacity. Determine if you have the resources required to support expansion.

7. Customer Segmentation:
Identify different customer segments and their unique needs. Determine if new services cater to existing customers or target new demographics.

8. Pilot Testing:
Consider pilot testing new services or expansions on a smaller scale before fully committing. This allows you to gauge customer response and iron out any challenges.

9. SWOT Analysis:
Conduct a SWOT (Strengths, Weaknesses, Opportunities, Threats) analysis to assess how new offerings align with your business's strengths and mitigate potential risks.

10. Scalability:
Evaluate whether the expansion or new services can be scaled without compromising quality. Ensure you can maintain consistency as you grow.

11. Legal and Regulatory Considerations:
Research any legal or regulatory requirements that may arise from offering new services or expanding your business.

12. Brand Alignment:
Ensure that new services or expansion opportunities align with your brand identity and reputation. Consistency is key to maintaining customer trust.

13. Customer Demand Testing:

Introduce the idea of new services to your existing customers through surveys or direct communication. Their response can indicate potential interest.

14. Strategic Partnerships:
Explore partnerships with suppliers, manufacturers, or complementary businesses that can support your expansion plans.

15. Return on Investment (ROI):
Calculate the potential ROI for each expansion or new service. Evaluate how long it will take to recoup your investment and start generating profits.

16. Long-Term Viability:
Consider the long-term viability of new services or expansion opportunities. Will they remain relevant as the industry evolves?

By following these steps, you can effectively evaluate the potential for expansion and additional service offerings in your mobile car detailing business. Thoughtful analysis, customer insights, and strategic planning will guide your decision-making process and set the foundation for successful growth.

Exploring Partnerships With Local Businesses And Dealerships

Exploring partnerships with local businesses and dealerships can be mutually beneficial for your mobile car detailing business. Here's a guide to help you establish and nurture these partnerships effectively:

1. Identify Potential Partners:
Research local businesses and dealerships that align with your target audience and services. Look for those that share a similar customer base.

2. Understand Their Needs:
Analyze what these businesses and dealerships might need from a car detailing service. It could be enhancing customer experience, maintaining

vehicle aesthetics, or improving vehicle resale value.

3. Tailor Your Pitch:
Craft a tailored pitch that outlines how your services can address their specific needs and add value to their customers.

4. Networking and Introduction:
Attend local networking events, business gatherings, or industry seminars to meet potential partners face-to-face. Introduce yourself and your services.

5. Start Small:
Begin with smaller collaborations or trial partnerships to build trust and showcase the benefits of working together.

6. Offer Value Proposition:
Clearly communicate the benefits of partnering with your mobile car detailing business, such as discounted rates for their customers or personalized service packages.

7. Collaborative Promotions:
Plan joint promotional activities that benefit both parties. For example, offer exclusive discounts to their customers in exchange for promoting your services.

8. Show Your Expertise:
Share your expertise in car detailing and how it aligns with their industry. Provide insights into how well-maintained vehicles can impact their business.

9. Provide Testimonials:
Share positive reviews and testimonials from satisfied customers to build credibility and demonstrate the quality of your services.

10. Demonstrate Professionalism:
Present yourself professionally during meetings and interactions. Your demeanor and approach can impact their perception of your business.

11. Personalized Approach:
Customize your approach for each potential partner. Understand their unique challenges and tailor your solutions accordingly.

12. Collaborative Marketing:
Co-create marketing materials or campaigns that highlight the partnership. This could include joint social media posts, blog articles, or event participation.

13. Build Relationships:
Focus on building strong relationships with your partners. Maintain open communication and provide exceptional service to strengthen the partnership.

14. Attend Local Events:
Participate in community events, fairs, or car shows where local businesses and dealerships are present. This provides opportunities for casual interactions.

15. Feedback and Continuous Improvement:
Listen to their feedback and suggestions for improvement. Adapt your services based on their insights to strengthen the partnership.

16. Measure Results:
Regularly evaluate the success of your partnerships based on metrics such as customer referrals, increased business, and customer satisfaction.

By approaching local businesses and dealerships with a genuine desire to add value to their operations, you can establish fruitful partnerships that contribute to the growth and success of your mobile car detailing business.

Leveraging Technology And Innovation To Stay Competitive In The Long Run

Leveraging technology and innovation is crucial for maintaining competitiveness and long-term success in your mobile car detailing business. Here's a comprehensive approach to stay ahead by embracing technology:

1. Stay Updated on Industry Trends:
Continuously monitor advancements in car detailing technology and industry trends. Stay informed about new tools, products, and techniques.

2. Digital Presence:
Build and maintain a professional website, social media profiles, and online booking systems. A strong online presence enhances your visibility and accessibility.

3. Mobile Apps:
Develop a mobile app for your business that allows customers to schedule appointments, receive updates, and access loyalty programs.

4. Online Booking and Payments:
Implement an online booking system and offer digital payment options for seamless customer interactions.

5. Customer Relationship Management (CRM) Software:
Use CRM software to manage customer data, preferences, and service histories for personalized interactions.

6. Automation Tools:
Automate repetitive tasks such as appointment reminders, follow-ups, and customer feedback collection.

7. High-Quality Equipment:
Invest in advanced detailing equipment that improves efficiency and enhances the quality of your services.

8. Waterless and Eco-Friendly Solutions:
Embrace eco-friendly practices by using waterless cleaning solutions and products that are environmentally responsible.

9. Detailing Software:
Utilize specialized detailing software to manage appointments, track inventory, and analyze business performance.

10. Online Training and Learning Platforms:
Offer online training for your team to stay updated on the latest detailing techniques and best practices.

11. Mobile Payments:
Offer mobile payment options that allow customers to pay on-site via digital wallets or credit cards.

12. Vehicle Tracking:
Use GPS tracking for your mobile vehicles to optimize routes, monitor locations, and improve scheduling efficiency.

13. Virtual Reality (VR) Demonstrations:
Use VR to provide virtual demonstrations of your services, helping customers visualize the results before committing.

14. Customer Feedback Analysis:
Use sentiment analysis tools to gauge customer satisfaction from online reviews and social media mentions.

15. Continuous Learning and Innovation:
Encourage a culture of continuous learning among your team members. Stay open to exploring new technologies that enhance your services.

16. Data Analytics:
Utilize data analytics to track customer preferences, service trends, and business performance. This informs strategic decisions.

17. Collaborations and Partnerships:
Collaborate with tech companies or startups that offer innovative solutions for the car care industry.

By embracing technology and innovation, you can streamline operations, enhance customer experiences, and position your mobile car detailing business as a leader in the industry. Regularly assess the relevance of new technologies to your business, test and implement the most suitable ones, and remain adaptable to changes in the digital landscape.

CONCLUSION

"As you reach the end of "Lather, Rinse, Succeed: Master The Art of Mobile Car Detailing," you've unlocked a treasure trove of insights, strategies, and inspiration to fuel your journey. From the first pages where you envisioned your dream to the final chapter where you're poised to take action, this book has been your trusted companion on the road to entrepreneurship.

Remember, success in the mobile car detailing industry is not just about wax and polish—it's about commitment, dedication, and an unwavering drive to deliver exceptional experiences. As you embark on this exciting venture, carry with you the lessons learned, the expert advice absorbed, and the belief that you have the tools to conquer challenges and realize your aspirations.

The road ahead may have twists and turns, but armed with a solid business plan, a passion for excellence, and the entrepreneurial spirit that led you here, you're well-equipped to navigate the path to success. Your journey has just begun, and we're excited to witness your growth, innovation, and impact in the dynamic world of mobile car detailing.

So, step confidently into this new chapter, embrace every opportunity, and let your dedication and hard work drive you towards unparalleled achievements. Your journey is one of passion, possibility, and boundless potential—may it be marked by the satisfaction of turning dreams into reality.

Congratulations on taking the first step toward becoming a driving force in the mobile car detailing industry. Here's to your unwavering commitment, your thriving business, and the road to 'Driven Success'!"

And as an added bonus, scan the QR code below and get a lifetime coupon of 10% off any t-shirt purchase. Simply apply the code BOOK at checkout.

9 798215 320532